Parks Are to Share

Parks Are to Share

a building block book

Lee Sullivan Hill

Carolrhoda Books, Inc./Minneapolis

For Colin, who loves parks of all kinds—Mom

For metric conversion, when you know the number of acres, multiply by .4 to find the number of hectares. When you know the number of square miles, multiply by 2.6 to find the number of square kilometers.

The photographs in this book are reproduced through the courtesy of: © David Jensen, front cover; © Steven Ferry, back cover, p. 5; © Wolfgang Kaehler 1997, pp. 1, 2, 6, 7, 15; © Buddy Mays/Travelstock, pp. 8, 12, 28, 29; © Don Eastman, p. 9; Tropix/© Christian Smith, p. 10; © Richard B. Levine, pp. 11, 23; © Bob Firth, p. 13; © Jerry Hennen, pp. 14, 21; © James P. Rowan, pp. 16, 20; © Mickey Pfleger, pp. 17, 27; © Phil Lauro, p. 18; © Jack Olson, p. 19; © Frank S. Balthis, pp. 22, 25; © Tom Pantages, pp. 24, 26.

Carolrhoda Books, Inc., c/o The Lerner Publishing Group
241 First Avenue North, Minneapolis, MN 55401 U.S.A.

Library of Congress Cataloging-in-Publication Data

Hill, Lee Sullivan, 1958–
    Parks are to share / Lee Sullivan Hill.
        p.   cm. — (A building block book)
    Includes index.
    Summary: Explains what a park is, how and why parks are built or preserved, and why parks are important to us, using examples from different parks from around the country.
    ISBN 1-57505-068-4
    1. Parks—Juvenile literature. [1. Parks.] I. Title. II. Series: Hill, Lee Sullivan, 1958– Building block book.
SB481.H45 1997
363.6'8—dc21   96-37457

Manufactured in the United States of America
1 2 3 4 5 6 – SP – 02 01 00 99 98 97

Parks are for fun. They give us swing sets and sand, tunnels and slides.

Parks give us natural beauty. They keep wild
places wild.

Parks give us green grass in the middle of the
city and quiet spaces to think and wonder.

What were parks like long ago? Wooded parks
held deer for kings and queens to hunt. Walls
around the woods kept most people out.

Ordinary people met in town squares.
Farmers came on market day to sell goods.
Barefoot children raced through the crowd
until it was time to go home.

Parks for all people opened in the 1800s.
One of the first was Birkenhead Park in England.
There, city children could play tag on grassy
fields, away from crowded streets.

A young American named Frederick Law
Olmsted visited Birkenhead. A few years later,
he helped build Central Park. It gave fresh
country air, woods, and ponds to people in
New York City.

Some people thought a park should have more than grass and trees. They wanted rides, food, and beaches. Amusement parks were born.

At an amusement park, you can ride a roller coaster or zoom down a water slide. How loudly can you scream?

Everyone has a different idea of what a park should be. Should it have grassy fields or scary rides? Should trees or sculpture frame the sky?

Parks can be wide-open spaces like Glacier
National Park.

They can be tiny, cozy spots like this "pocket" park. A wall of water hushes the sounds of Seattle all around.

Some parks are calm and quiet. Glide across the
water on a swan boat in Boston Public Garden.

Ballparks are loud! Cheer for the home team
and go for a hot dog at Candlestick Park.

Some parks are close. You can fly down a hill
on your sled in a park and still be home for dinner.

Others are far. You can get away for a week to
Yosemite National Park. Hike along the Merced
River. Wake up in a tent and cook breakfast
outside in the chill morning air.

The battlefield at Gettysburg is a national
military park. Why is it called a park? It helps us
remember the Civil War. It preserves history.

Everglades National Park preserves wild spaces
in Florida. Will you bring your children here to
see alligators someday?

Big and small. Near and far. All parks are different. They are also the same.

All are places to get away from the everyday. All are open to the public. And all take work.

Even before a park is built, people work.
First, they must find a place to put the park.
Some cities use an empty lot.

Next come thinking and planning. Who will
play in this park? Where will they sit?

Using the plans, workers shape the land. They plant trees and lay stones for walkways. They build ramps and railings and slippery slides.

Soon the park opens. But there's more work
to be done. Who will empty the trash or cut the
grass? Workers maintain parks. Volunteers help.

You can take care of parks, too. Pick up trash you see lying around. Walk on the paths so you don't hurt the grass. Join with your friends to keep your park beautiful.

When you grow up, you could plan new parks. You could be a builder and work on playgrounds. Or you could be a ranger and spend every day at a park.

Get away to a park. Swing and jump and run
at a park. Watch the fireworks on the Fourth of
July. Or just sit in a tree and read a good book.

Parks let us think and dream and smile.

Parks are for people to share.

A Photo Index to the Parks in This Book

 **Cover** The United States shares the beauties of Grand Teton National Park in Wyoming with visitors from many places. Two visiting pelicans float in the Snake River.

 **Page 1** Canoes await the day's paddlers on the shore of Lake Louise. The lake is located in Banff National Park, high up in the Canadian Rockies in Alberta.

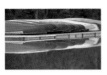 **Page 2** You can see all the way to another country from this Canadian park! The park is in Windsor, Ontario, Canada. Look for the skyscrapers of Detroit, Michigan, across the water.

 **Page 5** City and town parks often include playgrounds with slides and swings. New playgrounds are designed with ramps, too, so that children in wheelchairs can also share in the fun.

 **Page 6** Canada has preserved more than 2,500 square miles of wilderness in Banff National Park. This beautiful land is home to elk, bighorn sheep, mountain goats, marmots, pikas, wildcats, and bears.

 **Page 7** This is Dorchester Square, part of Heartland Park in Montreal, Quebec, Canada. You could sit under a big, shady tree here and read a book—maybe *The Park Book*, written by Charlotte Zolotow and illustrated by H. A. Rey.

 **Page 8** Kings and queens have lived at Windsor Castle near London, England, for hundreds of years. Windsor Great Park, which surrounds the castle, covers 4,000 acres and has its own herd of red deer.

 **Page 9** Climb up and up the stairs of the city tower in Innsbruck, Austria. You can see the square down below. It hasn't changed much since the Middle Ages.

 **Page 10** Tag, you're it! There are still meadows to run across at Birkenhead Park near Liverpool, England. Sir Joseph Paxton planned the park. It opened in 1847.

 **Page 11** Frederick Law Olmsted and Calvert Vaux planned Central Park in New York City. Vaux designed the stairways, bridges, and buildings. Olmsted planned the trees, ponds, and pathways—all part of the park's landscape. Olmsted was the first person to call himself a landscape architect.

 **Page 12** Amusement parks became popular at the end of the 1800s when train and trolley lines were opened. People could get out of the city for a day of fun. Would you like to ride the roller coaster at this modern amusement park in San Antonio, Texas?

 **Page 13** Sculpture sprouts like plants outside the Walker Art Center in Minneapolis, Minnesota. Artists Claes Oldenburg and Coosje van Bruggen placed *Spoonbridge and Cherry* in the sculpture garden—it didn't grow there.

 **Page 14** Wildflowers decorate Logan Pass in Glacier National Park in Montana. Although it's summer, snow still covers the mountaintops nearby.

 **Page 15** Landscape architects tuck "pocket" parks into small city spaces. Waterfall Garden Park fits into a nook in downtown Seattle, Washington.

 **Page 16** The swan boats in Boston Public Garden glide quietly because they have no motors. Each boat's driver (in the swan) pedals a waterwheel. Author Robert McCloskey made the swan boats famous worldwide in his book *Make Way for Ducklings*.

 **Page 17** In 1960, the San Francisco Giants began playing their home baseball games in this ballpark named Candlestick Park.

 **Page 18** Parks are fun any time of year. In winter, people bundle up to skate, ski, and sled in many parks.

 **Page 19** The Merced River flows through Yosemite Valley, in the mountains of California. Wild places such as Yosemite National Park do not always look this peaceful on busy summer weekends. Should the National Park Service let everyone enjoy nature or limit visitors to keep the peace? There is no easy answer.

 **Page 20** Visitors remember the Battle of Gettysburg at Gettysburg National Military Park in Pennsylvania. These men are dressed like sharpshooters who fought in the battle in 1863.

 **Page 21** Everglades National Park in Florida is home to many endangered species. How many alligators can you see?

 **Page 22** You can visit a Dutch windmill and a Japanese teahouse without leaving San Francisco. Both are found in Golden Gate Park.

 **Page 23** A loader clears a vacant lot in New York City. Back at the office, a landscape architect draws plans for the new park.

 **Page 24** Volunteers use a landscape architect's plans to build a new playground at White Park in the city of Concord, New Hampshire.

 **Page 25** A worker mows the grass at San Gregorio State Beach in California. Before lawn mowers were invented, some parks used sheep or even bison to cut the grass!

 **Page 26** The volunteers from page 24 are at it again! This time, they're raking leaves. How can you help out at your park?

 **Page 27** These rangers at Yosemite National Park patrol the wilderness on horseback. Would you like to be a park ranger?

 **Page 28** Fireworks light the sky at this park across the Mississippi River from Saint Louis, Missouri.

 **Page 29** These two young brothers share some time at a park in Upstate New York. They are fishing in one of the long, skinny lakes called the Finger Lakes.